MW00899303

John in Maze Land

Copyright 2024 Sooho Lee
All right reserved. This book or any portion there of
may not be reproduced or used in any manner whatsoever
without the express written permission of the publisher
except the use of brief quatations in a book review.

First Printing, 2024

StoryWalkers

John in Maze Land

written by Sooho Lee
Illustrated by Midjourney

John is a ten-year-old boy.

He has short straight hair.

He usually wears a black hoody
and black pants.

He enjoys adventures.

One day, John went to school.

He opened his school locker.

"Oh, what is it?" gasped John.

There was a deep hole in there.

It was a portal.

"Anyone in there?" asked John.

There was no answer.

John jumped into the portal.

"Ouch! Where am I?" said John.
He looked around.
He was in the maze.
Just then, a big eagle flew over to him.
John ran away and fell into a hole.

"Phew, now where am I?" asked John.

He was in a cave.

"Pssss."

He heard a sound and looked down at his feet.

"Yikes!" shrieked John.

There was an enormous snake in the cave.

John ran away.

The ground was wobbling.

"Awww!"

John was in a muddy swamp.

He saw a huge crocodile.

"Yikes!" yelled John.

He swam as fast as possible.

He managed to get out of the swamp.

John arrived at a castle.

He opened the gate and walked in there.

There was a staircase.

He walked upstairs.

He reached the castle tower.

There was a big dragon.

It stared at John and roared.

John ran down the stairs,

and the dragon chased after him.

He went into a storeroom and closed the door.

"Phew!" sighed John.

A wizard appeared.

He was an old man wearing a blue hat

and a blue gown.

"You are such a brave boy.

Let me give you magic potions.

Use this potion when you are in danger,"

said the wizard.

"Oh, thank you!" said John.

John left the castle.

The dragon flew after him.

The Evil was riding the dragon.

"Oh, no!" said John.

"Catch him!" said the Evil.

The Evil was riding the dragon.

"Get him!" cried the Evil.

John ran and ran.

The dragon was getting closer to him.

"Oh, I'm in danger!" thought John.

He had an idea.

He had the magic potion that the wizard

had given him.

He held the potion in the air.

"Help me!"

Then, a portal appeared.

John jumped into the portal.

John was back to school.

"Oops! I'm late!" said John.

He hurried to his classroom.

He opened the door.

"Sorry, I'm late!"

John smiled.

Sooho Lee

Hello, my name is Sooho Lee.

I'm ten years old.

I live in Busan, South Korea.

I like to read books.

I enjoy reading adventure stories.

I wrote this story about a boy named John and his adventure in the maze.

I hope you enjoy reading my book.

Made in the USA
Columbia, SC
07 April 2024

33908111R00015